OMAN

A PICTORIAL TOUR

OMAN
A PICTORIAL TOUR

JAAP CROESE

MOTIVATE
PUBLISHING

Acknowledgements

The author would like to thank Nella Croese for her assistance in writing the captions for this book; Cathryn Ashton, for her patience and company during the many photo trips they made together; Vincent van Engelen for supplying the superb image of the Majlis al-Jinn on page 101; Dr Patricia Groves for her valuable advice; and the friends who helped him bring this book to fruition.

Published by Motivate Publishing

Dubai: PO Box 2331, Dubai, UAE
Tel: (+971 4) 282 4060, fax: (+971 4) 282 7898
e-mail: books@motivate.ae   www.booksarabia.com

Office 508, Building No 8, Dubai Media City, Dubai, UAE
Tel: (+971 4) 390 3550, fax: (+971 4) 390 4845

Abu Dhabi: PO Box 43072, Abu Dhabi, UAE
Tel: (+971 2) 677 2005, fax: (+971 2) 677 0124

London: Acre House, 11/15 William Road, London NW1 3ER
e-mail: motivateuk@motivate.ae

Directors: Obaid Humaid Al Tayer
                        Ian Fairservice

Consultant Editor: David Steele
Editors: Pippa Sanderson
                        Moushumi Nandy
Art Director: Andrea Willmore
Senior Designer: Cithadel Francisco

General Manager Books: Jonathan Griffiths
Publishing Coordinator: Zelda Pinto

© Jaap Croese and Motivate Publishing 2006

Reprinted 2007, 2008

ISBN: 978 1 86063 174 0

British Library Cataloguing-in-Publication Data. A catalogue record for this book is available from the British Library.

Printed by Rashid Printers, Ajman, UAE

Originally published
with the support of

The Wave
MUSCAT
www.thewavemuscat.com

FOREWORD

by Dr Rajiha Abdul-Ameer Ali
Minister of Tourism, Sultanate of Oman

If you flip through these pages that detail the beauty and splendour of Oman, you'll realize a tremendous amount of energy and time has gone into producing this spectacular pictorial voyage. *Oman – A Pictorial Tour* will go far in enlightening tourists and, in fact, the world, about the hidden treasures the Sultanate of Oman has to offer.

Oman is an alluring travel destination, featuring an attractive tourism package that is an ideal mix of adventure, culture and arts. It's a blend of seemingly endless desert expanses, virgin beaches and a beautiful, lush southern region while, at the same time, the country's historical significance is amplified by the presence of more than 500 forts, castles and watchtowers. *Oman – A Pictorial Tour* brings forth the diversity of Oman through an incomparable collection of spectacular photographs.

The government has pledged its complete support for the growth of sustainable tourism in the Sultanate, given its splendid landscape, mesmerising beauty, heritage and well-developed infrastructure. Leading integrated tourism resorts such as The Wave, Muscat, which has sponsored *Oman – A Pictorial Tour*, have added impetus to Oman's growing appeal as a unique tourism destination. On behalf of the government, I would also like to congratulate everyone associated with this project for bringing out this beautiful pictorial showcase of Oman.

Rajiha

INTRODUCTION

The longer I live in the Sultanate of Oman, the more the culture, landscape, flora and fauna reveal themselves in all their beauty and richness. This book is the result of many years of photography, with the help of the people of Oman who, once they got to know me, were always willing to share the most beautiful and interesting treasures in their neighbourhoods. Their hospitality is something you cannot capture in a picture, but was critical in the photography you see before you.

Travelling round Oman and taking photographs was like a journey into the unknown. It was never possible to foresee how a trip would end, what I would encounter and what the results would be. Each one of Oman's eight main regions has its own highlights – be it the date harvest, the exquisite beauty of the forts and the history they represent, the coastal views and marine life, the dhows and their construction, the craft workshops, the atmospheric souks or the colourful dresses of the Omani women. All have their own tales of beauty.

Omani civilization dates back at least 7,000 years, and it is the remnants of this past, along with Oman's natural beauty, that is drawing tourists from round the globe. While Oman's natural wonders are a significant factor in attracting visitors, the country is developing tourism while maintaining its natural surroundings. Integrated developments such as The Wave, Muscat epitomize the country's rich architectural heritage.

A beautiful landscape sustains the quality of life for all who live and work within it, encouraging their sense of ownership and pride. The prime objective of this book is to salute the Omani people and their rich and colourful heritage and culture, and to encourage visitors to respect what they see.

The Omani culture is unspoilt and not one that should be compared with Western customs and values. Such richness needs to be explored with the respect and care it deserves and this, in turn, will enhance the wonderful experience Oman has to offer.

I would like to dedicate this book to everyone in the Sultanate of Oman who has contributed to it in their own way.

Jaap Croese

6

Previous spread: The Musandam Peninsula is known as the 'Norway of Arabia' and is located in the northernmost part of Oman, separated from the rest of the Sultanate by the northerly extension of the UAE. Oman has been a seafaring nation for thousands of years; in fact, as far back as the 8th-century AD, an Omani vessel is known to have reached Canton in China. Traditional dhows, including the *Boum*, *Ghanjah*, *Shu'i* and *Badan*, to name but a few types, were used in trading and could weather most storms safely.

Above: Local fishermen in Musandam spread their catch of sardines on the beach to dry. The dried fish is used as animal fodder.

Right: The water pipe used for smoking aromatic tobacco is known by several names, including the *shisha*, *hookah* and *argilah*. The pipe filters and cools the smoke from tobacco, which is burned on charcoal. *Shisha* tobacco flavours are made from fruit such as apple, strawberry, mango and apricot, or from other pleasant sources such as honey and mint.

Above: A boy from the *Shihuh* tribe in Musandam holds up a *jirz,* a small axe with a decorated blade, which is carried instead of the usual curved *khanjar* dagger found elsewhere in the Sultanate. This weapon is unique to the area, a result of the peninsula's isolation from the rest of the country.

Top right: *Jirz* handles are made from the *Lotus jujube* or *mazj* tree.

Bottom right: Bukha Fort, a small fort with an unusual pear-shaped watchtower, is surrounded on three sides by a dry moat. Its entrance is flanked by cannons, which are fired towards the sea when the moon is sighted at the end of Ramadan, signalling the beginning of Eid celebrations.

Nimble Iranian speedboats, with outboard motors, prepare to leave Khasab
for the short trip to Iran, while the traditional *Sambuq* (a form of dhow)
offers visitors a glimpse into life onboard an historic Arabian trading vessel.

Almost the entire 650 kilometres of the Musandam coast features coves, fjords and islands, which offer many opportunities for exploration, both above and below the water. You may even see dolphins or green turtles.

The Batinah coast runs from Khatmat al-Malaha in the north to the Muscat region in the south. With a coastal plain some 25 kilometres wide, the Batinah region lies at the foot of the Western Hajar Mountains; and, after Muscat, it is the most densely inhabited area in Oman. The area has a long history of maritime and industrial activity. In particular the fish souk by the beach gives the village of Barka a good livelihood. In the heart of Barka, you will find an abundance of fresh fish, with varieties ranging from tuna to sardines. If you arrive before 10.00 am, you are likely to see a fish auction, which is always a lively and interesting spectacle. The weighted rope of a medium gauge cast net, right, is made of goat hair, a plentiful material in Oman.

Above: An old house, Bait al-Ras, in the village of Al-Ulyah in Wadi Bani Kharus, is fortified against attack by its elevation and thick walls.

Right: Forts and castles are a main attraction of the Batinah. The wadis are also very popular, especially Wadi Bani Ghafar, Wadi Al-Sahtan and Wadi Bani Awf. Pictured here is the head of Wadi Bani Awf, where the picturesque mountain village of Bilad Sayt, hugging the mountainside, is accessed along a precipitous road.

18

Above: The Batinah plain is known as the breadbasket of Oman and has been cultivated for centuries with a variety of food crops. A visit to Wadi Mistal to see the plantations in the mountain village of Wakan is well worth the trip, as grapes, apricots, pomegranates and bananas are grown in a truly beautiful setting. In Spring, the apricot and almond blossoms attract hundreds of visitors. The scene of white and pink blossoms in fields of green against a backdrop of dark grey mountains crowning the Ghubra Bowl, is spectacular.

Left: Oman's 11,000 *falaj* form a large interconnected system of water channels used for irrigation and to transport water from the mountaintops and wadis over long distances, for a variety of purposes.

Above: A major landmark on the Batinah coast, Barka Castle is only a few hundred metres from the shore of the Gulf of Oman. It features an unusual octagonal tower and, to the rear of the castle, are two restored watchtowers which were once part of the town's defensive wall. A bustling vegetable and fish souk between the castle and the beach gives Barka a lively atmosphere.

Right: One cannot miss the impressive sight of Nakhal Fort, spectacularly perched on a rocky prominence amid date-palm trees in the foothills of the Western Hajar Mountains. Some 350 years old, the fort played an important role in the defensive system of the country as it guarded precious water resources and controlled the passage to the Interior. The fort's six towers were added in stages by successive generations. In 1990 the fort was restored using traditional materials. Nakhal is also famous for its perennial, mineral-laden hot springs, which flow from mountain clefts.

These beautiful old houses can be found in the village of Al-Ulyah in Wadi Bani Kharus. For several centuries, the village has overlooked the valley, guarding it in the interest of safe passage, especially in more dangerous times.

Above: The *habban*, or bag pipe, was introduced into Oman quite recently, a legacy of His Majesty Sultan Qaboos bin Said's sojourn with the Scottish Cameronian regiment in the late 1960s.

Top left: Omanis take great pride in their horses, which symbolise the nobility and longevity of their culture. The Oman Equestrian Federation arranges race meetings and equestrian events to perpetuate this aspect of their heritage.

Bottom left: Camel racing is a very intense, traditional Bedouin activity. Race meets occur throughout the country and big prizes are frequently on offer. Pampered racing camels are fed dates, clover, alfalfa and oats; and, just before a race, many are given milk, honey and dates to enhance their performance.

Traditional Omani dancing during a camel-racing event. The men perform the stick dance, or *ayala*, while young girls swirl their hair to the rhythm.

Muscat has retained its Old-World character. Oman's capital, nestled at the foot of the Eastern Hajar Mountains, is a city of white buildings, beautiful minarets and well-manicured roadsides containing flowers of all colours.

Above: Old Muscat has a romantic charm, and is graced with many forts, castles, mosques and towers. Of particular note are Mirani Fort, top, and Jalali Fort, above, which flank Al-Alam Palace of His Majesty Sultan Qaboos.

Left: The sprawling Ruwi area of Muscat, nestled within the mountain folds, and viewed from the elevated road to the coastal town of Yitti.

Above: His Majesty Sultan Qaboos bin Said's Al-Alam Palace in old Muscat is a unique structure rendered in a modern Arabian architectural style, featuring tall arches and pillars in gold and blue. It was completed in the 1970s as a symbol of Oman's Renaissance and is used mainly for ceremonial functions.

Right: Elegant merchant houses with gracefully carved wooden balconies line the waterfront of Matrah Corniche, their façades masking the maze of alleyways in Souk al-Zalam. The minaret rising over the rooftops belongs to the Al-Rasool al-Adham mosque with its iconic blue, purple and gold dome.

Above: Sultan Qaboos University opened in 1986. It now has seven colleges offering degrees in a range of programmes, including Education, Commerce, Science, Agriculture, Arts, Engineering and Medicine. The landscaping for the university was designed to create the feeling of a traditional oasis settlement with hidden gardens and a surrounding defensive wall.

Right: The twin forts of Mirani and Jalali guard the ancient harbour of Muscat from opposite sides. Between them lies the harbour with the Al-Alam Palace on the central shore. The forts are strategically positioned on the rocky hilltops of the western and eastern flanks of this perfect horseshoe harbour. Both forts were built in the 16th century by the Portuguese using the foundations and structures of original Omani citadels. Mirani Fort, which contains what is thought to be the oldest chapel in the Gulf, was completed circa 1587. In the foreground of this picture stands the Al-Khawr mosque, with its distinctive blue and gold domes.

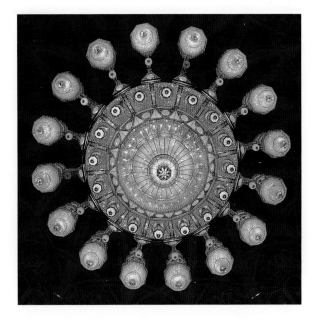

The Sultan Qaboos Grand Mosque is situated along the main highway between the city of Muscat and its airport at Seeb. The mosque is built on an elevated podium amid vast gardens. A gift of His Majesty Sultan Qaboos bin Said to the people of Oman, this very elegant mosque is of unsurpassed beauty. The mosque has the capacity for 20,000 worshippers, but is not only a place of worship. It is also a seat for Islamic learning, with a comprehensive library and an Institute for Islamic Studies. An enormous Persian carpet covers the entire floor of the main prayer hall in a single piece, 70 x 60 metres in size. The carpet, rendered in lovely floral and arabesque patterns with an array of colours including golden beige, deep blue and red madder, took 600 dedicated weavers four years to complete. Above the carpet hangs the world's largest chandelier made of Austrian Swarovski crystal and gold plate with 1,122 lamps.

Left: The waters around Oman teem with colourful and varied marine life, such as this well camouflaged seahorse hiding among numerous featherstars.

Far left: A beautiful arch at Bandar Jissah with gently dipping tertiary sediments.

Below: Sailing is a popular pastime and regattas such as this one at Muscat are well attended by Omanis and expatriates alike.

Above: A small fishing village on the way to Seifa, past Bandar Khayran.

Left: Seifa Beach is on a beautiful, pristine shore just an hour from the capital city of Muscat. While fishermen prepare their catch, a trio of flamingoes strolls along, watching from the shoreline.

Left: Cycling along the scenic coastal road from Qurayyat to Sur.

Below: Wadi Suwayh, a world away from the hubbub of the capital, is an idyllic spot with calm blue pools. The area is one of the most scenic in the Eastern Hajar Mountains. Ramblers will have an excellent day's adventure if they walk from the nearby village of Suwayh.

Far left: An aerial shot of the Bandar Kharan coastline. Oman's mountains are the result of a collision of the continental and oceanic tectonic plates some 60-million years ago, which caused major earth movements, resulting in the uplift of sedimentary mountains all along the northern coast and into the south-western spine of Oman.

Above: Attractive Marina Bandar al-Rowdha, situated close to the Al-Bustan Palace Hotel in Sidab, is one of Muscat's premier attractions. It is a purpose-built water-sports complex offering a variety of marine-related activities and charters, including yachting, snorkelling, scuba-diving, sport-fishing and dolphin and whale-watching trips.

Top left: Catering to the Sultanate's growing tourism industry, Shangri-La's Barr al-Jissah Resort & Spa is located on an azure bay, half an hour's drive east from Muscat. Against a dramatic mountain backdrop in yellow ochre, the three large hotel complexes are spread along a curving beach of pure white sand.

Bottom left: The Al-Bustan Palace Hotel, 10 minutes from Old Muscat, is set like a jewel in 200 acres of private gardens, with a beautiful crescent beach and turquoise waters against a jagged ring of exotic black mountains.

This spread: The Muscat Festival is a colourful and exciting event, which is hosted at various locations around the capital. Held during January and February each year, it has a heritage theme with a rich variety of amusements and activities especially for families with children.

Following spread: An old man offers camel loading straps of braided wool for sale during the Muscat Festival. These straps are ideal as key rings. A woman plaits the end of a short warp-faced camel girth strap made of cotton and metallic threads, designed to appeal to festival visitors.

Folklore dancers from the Batinah region provide entertainment for the crowd during the Muscat Festival. In the above picture, a dancer warms the goat-skin membrane of his drum against the fire, so that it will emit richer tones.

The National Day celebrations in November are always spectacular and, in 2005, they were even more sensational and visually impressive as they celebrated His Majesty Sultan Qaboos bin Said's 35th year of rule. In the picture on the left, the colours worn by the school children seated in the background form letters which wish the Sultan happy birthday in Arabic.

Whether by night or day, the old harbour town of Matrah with its corniche, its elegant old buildings and central mosque is a picturesque sight. Matrah is home to the famous Matrah Souk which is many centuries old. Fronted on the corniche, the souk covers a wide area with row upon row of shops selling all manner of goods, including frankincense, spices, dates and a plethora of antiques. This time-honoured souk has maintained its traditional character and plays a unique role in the capital area as a bustling commercial centre and cultural repository.

Above: Children on their way home from school in the Interior town of Ibri.

Right: The Dhahirah region encompasses a desert plain extending from the Western Hajar Mountains towards The Empty Quarter in the south. The region is known for its oil and gas reserves, as well as for its archaeological sites. The grave structures at Bat, Al-Khutm and Al-Ayn have been inscribed as a World Heritage Site by UNESCO. Twenty 5,000-year-old, free-standing 'beehive' tombs line a ridge above Wadi al-Ayn, with Jebel Mischt providing a majestic backdrop.

Sulaif is a classic, small, fortified town containing a fort, mosque, souk and residential quarters, perched on a plateau above a wadi plain. Though in ruins the town, in its majestic setting, still has a noble air. Built by Imam Sultan bin Saif al Yaarubi in 1718 AD, the stone and red-mud buildings blend harmoniously with the mountains behind. In the picture above, the trading town of Ibri is visible in the distance, revealing Sulaif's strategic location.

Above: A man from Ibri returns home to his family with goods from a neighbouring souk, his camels laden with bread and rice. Note that this solitary rider keeps his camels together and maintains control of them with headstall equipment, known as *khatam*, and made of trappings, or straps secured around the neck and head of each camel.

Right: National Day celebrations are always an important event in the calendar and sometimes the main ceremony is held in one of the regions. Here we see celebrations underway in the Dhahirah region's principal town of Ibri.

After these large, *khalas* dates have been collected by boys, they're carefully sorted out by a group of women prior to being boiled in special date ovens. Typically, this time-honoured activity combines work with socializing and takes place during one week a year – usually early in July – before the dates have fully ripened.

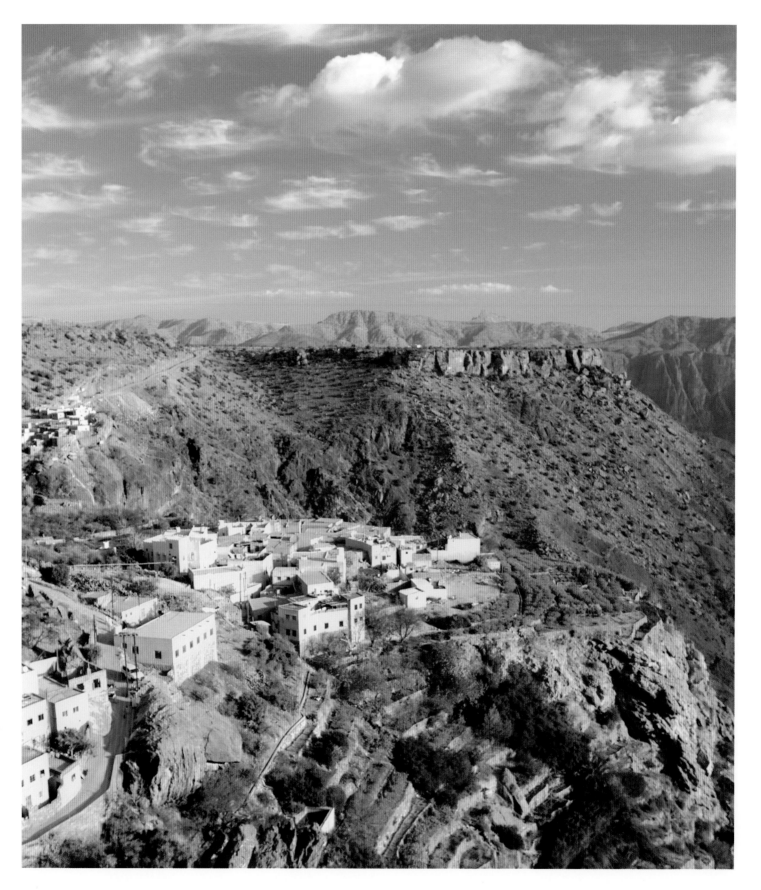

The Dakhiliyah region contains a plethora of mountains, wadis and historical sites and is home to a number of traditional handicraft industries. Crowning the administrative capital of Nizwa is a great citadel with an iconic round tower dating from the 1650s. Peaks in the Jebel Akhdar or 'Green Mountain' range, so named because their rocky slopes have a greenish tone, rise to heights of some 3,000 metres, the highest in Oman. Terracing in the Sayq region of the Jebel Akhdar range, pictured above, is designed to capture rain as well as mineral-rich material eroded from the mountain rock. Cultivation includes vegetables, grain, animal fodder and exotic fruit.

Above: Water from Wadi Tanuf cascades into a *falaj* after heavy rainfall.

Left: The most valuable date crop, the *khalas*, thrives in the Interior. With 65 per cent sugar, it is one of the most delicious varieties of date. The fruit is bright yellow, oval in shape, and eaten either fresh or semi-dry.

Above: Al-Hoti Cave, in the Hajar Mountains near Jebel Akhdar, is an underground cavern with a subterranean lake system. The main chamber contains magnificent sculptures, with stalactites and stalagmites, and exotic formations that have taken millions of years to evolve. These beautiful structures are coloured in shades of pink, yellow, gold, beige and grey. The cave's freshwater lake, some 800-metres long, is home to a delicate ecosystem with unusual species, such as blind fish.

Right: Indian rollers add extra colour and vibrancy to the rich avifauna of Oman. They can be encountered in scrub and trees near the coast where they rest and feed before continuing their migratory journey. When in flight the roller's wings splash the air with brilliant blue and turquoise.

Above: A lone watchtower, or *burj*, stands guard over the well-maintained *falaj* system and accompanying date-palm plantation of Misfat al-Abreyeen, not far from the town of Al-Hamra.

Left: The Sama'il Gap has strategic importance as the only natural pass separating the Eastern from the Western Hajar Mountains. Throughout history, the gap provided a passage for goods and people to travel from Muscat and settlements in the Dakhiliyah region. Protected by the Sama'il Fort situated above the village, the gap was used to transport both local and imported goods.

A hamlet in the Jebel Akhdar range. These mountains were the scene of several skirmishes between the government and insurrectionists led by the defiant Suleiman bin Himyar, the 'Sheikh of the Green Mountain' in the late 1950s. Two squadrons of SAS, together with the Trucial Oman Scouts, fought the rebels for two years during what became known as the 'Jebel Akhdar Campaign'. In 1959, the rebels were forced to lay down their arms and peace returned to the region.

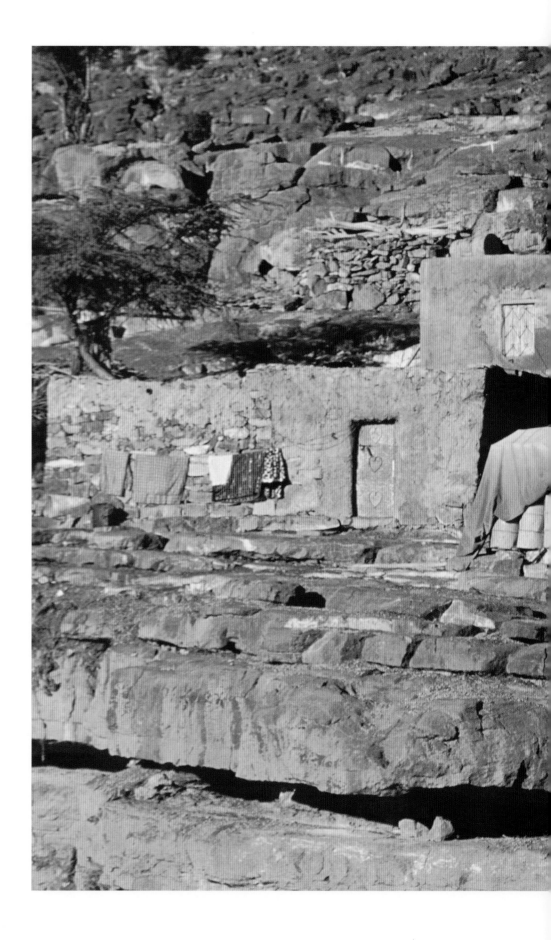

Above: It was in the village of Adam that Imam Ahmed bin Said, founder of the present ruling dynasty, was born. His home in Harrat al-Jamii, pictured here, remains open. Some of the original houses, though long since abandoned, remain relatively unchanged, with beautifully decorated walls and ceilings. Oman's old painted ceilings added grace and aesthetic interest to important rooms. Ceilings were supported by horizontal frameworks of palm tree wood and/or mangrove poles.

Left: Children help with domestic chores, such as washing dishes, shown here with boys and girls participating together in the endeavour.

One of the hallmarks of traditional architecture throughout the Sultanate is the beautiful carving of wooden doors and window frames, which incorporate Islamic, geometric and arabesque design work and can be seen gracing palaces, forts and mosques, and even the most modest of homes. The doors above right and opposite, are more recent products, manufactured from steel and colourfully decorated with floral motifs.

Above: An old mosque in a village in the Jebel Akhdar range. Although the mosque has seen better days, it is still in frequent use. Pictured is the prayer niche or *mihrab*, which indicates the direction of Mecca.

Right: The impressive new Sultan Qaboos mosque at Bahla.

80

Above: Both Musilmat on the coast and Bahla in the Interior are centres of comparatively high-volume pottery production, with large alluvial deposits of soil providing an abundant source of clay.

Left: Shepherds are adept at spinning in a standing position, or even while walking, as they tend their herds in the mountains.

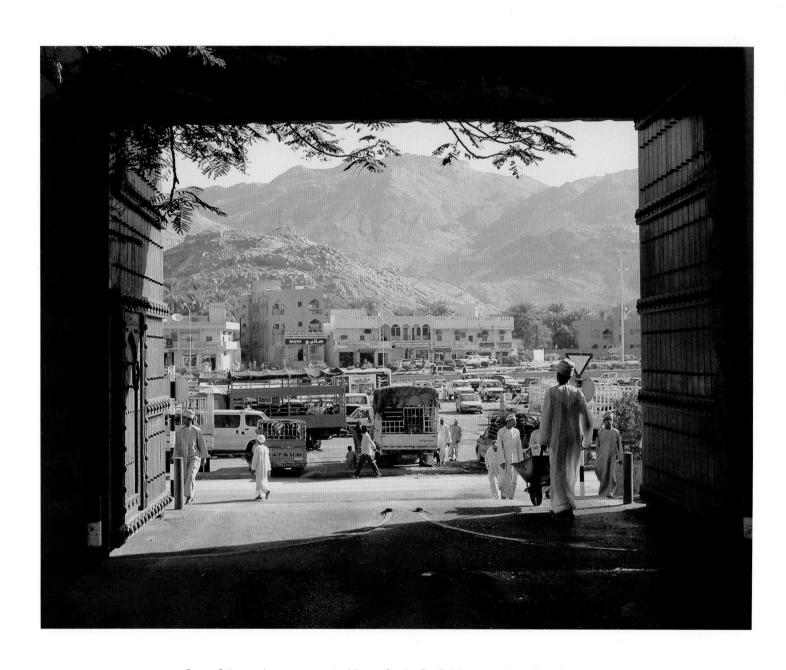

One of the main entrances to Nizwa Souk. On Friday mornings there's a bustling animal market, where cows, goats and sheep can be bought. In addition, the market features many handicrafts and there are also sections for fruit and vegetables, clothing and second-hand motor vehicles.

The Nizwa Friday or *juma* souk. In the background is the famous Nizwa Fort, which, in the past, was the scene of many battles. The well-preserved fort, with its enormous round tower, is an excellent example of the ingenuity of traditional Omani defensive architecture.

Nizwa Souk, with two youngsters repairing a bicycle. Though headwear fashion varies from region to region, generally Omani men and boys wear the *mussar* or turban for more formal occasions; and, for ordinary wear, they choose the *kummah*, a perforated cotton cap, which is quilted and embroidered with coloured cotton thread.

It's customary in many regions of Oman for women's clothing to encompass vibrant splashes of colour, embroidery and decoration. Clothing varies from region to region and is also linked to tribal traditions, with designs often fashioned to protect the skin from the elements and to store important items.

This spread: Time-etched faces speak of desert, sun and wind and of a harsh life in a country that, until 1970, had changed little since Medieval times.

Following spread: Fishermen from Tiwi use circular, weighted cast nets to catch sardines, anchovies and other small fish in the shallow coastal waters.

Above: Easily recognised by its distinctive stem at the bow and 'wings' at the stem, the *Shu'i* is the most common of traditional Omani boats. A jumble of wooden *Shu'i* can be seen drawn up on the shores of Al-Ayjah Bay, across the inlet from Sur. Although now overtaken by fibreglass copies, the *Shu'i* remains the workhorse of the Omani fishing industry. In the background on the wharf, an elaborate large *Sambuq* or wooden dhow is being built.

Right: Azure seas and virgin beaches are characteristic of the coast in the Sharqiyah region, complemented inland by dramatic gorges and serene wadis. The region also features desert dunes, oases and the busy city of Sur, an ancient ship-building centre on the Arabian Sea. Pictured, top, is the lighthouse at the village of Ayjah at Sur; and, bottom, the blue waters of the creek at Al-Ayjah Bay, historically a haven for traders.

Above: A night under the stars is one of the pleasures of holidaying in Oman. Although there are a few official campsites, there are plenty of places to camp within easy reach of Muscat. A 4x4 is usually necessary, as once you're off the main roads, tracks are usually impassable for saloon cars.

Top left: The turtle reaches maturity at about 30 years of age and the female may lay thousands of eggs during her lifetime, although not many of her hatchlings will survive to adulthood. In order to provide the hatchlings with the best possible chance, the government has banned camping on local beaches. However, you can witness newborn turtles racing towards the water if you obtain a special permit and are accompanied by an official. Five different species of turtles inhabit Omani waters, including the endangered Green Turtle pictured, the Loggerhead turtle, the Olive Ridley turtle and the critically endangered Hawksbill turtle. The Leatherback turtle remains offshore.

Bottom left: *Calidris Minuta*, the little stint, a winter migrant to the Sultanate.

The Sharqiyah Sands offer a romantic view of the desert, with rolling sand dunes that can rise to 100 metres. Reminiscent of ocean waves and varying from deep red to a rich honey colour, the sea of dunes stretches for some 180 kilometres from north to south and 80 kilometres from east to west.

Many tour operators will offer excursions to the Sharqiyah Sands as part of their holiday package, transporting guests in modern, air-conditioned 4x4s and visiting a Bedouin campsite, where the uninitiated can share a meal with local people and gain a taste of authentic desert life.

Above: Lying in a deep canyon gorge is Wadi Shab, one of Oman's most scenic wadis, with water all year round. Narrow, winding paths are edged with tall grasses, banana groves and mango trees. Emerald pools of water entice swimmers; and the famous keyhole passage leads to a magnificent cave with a waterfall that sparkles in shafts of sunlight. The brave can climb to the top and jump several metres into the shimmering water below.

Left: An Omani boy peers over the edge of the spectacular cliffs at Ra's al-Jinz, known locally as 'Turtle Beach'. This secluded, sandy beach provides ideal conditions for turtles to lay their eggs and the area is an important turtle-conservation project for the government.

Ninety tombs from the 3rd-millennium BC are found on a plateau in the Eastern Hajar Mountains. The tombs have survived remarkably well, perhaps because of good workmanship and their inaccessible location. They appear to have been about four- to five-metres high and three to four metres in diameter. Some are double walled and some possess two storeys. In one of the tombs, excavated in 1994, skeletal remains and burial goods, including fragments of pottery, were discovered.

At 60,000 square metres, the vast Majlis al-Jinn cave, in the Eastern Hajar Mountains, is a highlight in Oman's arsenal of caves and one of the largest underground chambers in the world. It offers some of the most exciting cave exploration anywhere. Meaning 'meeting place of the *djinns*' (folklore spirits), the Majlis al-Jinn is an extremely difficult cave to negotiate and should be attempted only with professional guidance. It has only one access and exit point, involving, on entry, a free abseil of 120–150 metres.

During the 14th and 15th centuries, one of the most important towns in the Sharqiyah region was Qalhat, which is located along the coast some 25 kilometres north-west of Sur. Ships sailed to India with cargoes of horses, dates, pearls and salt, returning with cloth, metalwork, spices and rice. The Arab traveller, Ibn Battuta, who visited Qalhat circa 1330 AD, wrote that the town possessed one of the most beautiful mosques in the world, with walls of blue ceramic tiles, built during the 2nd-century AD. However, Qalhat's days were numbered. An earthquake at the end of the 14th century is thought to have destroyed many of the town's fine buildings. In 1508 the Portuguese ransacked the town, killing much of the population and burning their boats and buildings. Today nothing remains except the ruins of the monument known as 'Bibi Maryam', pictured, the foundations of houses, the remains of a wall and an ancient cistern.

Above: Although donkeys have been replaced as beasts of burden by motor vehicles, it's still possible to witness the evocative sight portrayed here.

Left: An old man contemplates life under a tree in the Sharqiyah region.

Above: Sharqiyah Mountain tribe girls tending their goats. Livestock herding is a mainstay of rural and nomadic lifestyles throughout the Sultanate because the animals provide a ready supply of meat and dairy products, and their wool, hair and hides have many uses.

Right: Sharqiyah girls dressed traditionally for a social event.

Following spread: *Burqas* come in a variety of shapes, sizes and colours. Eyes rimmed with kohl and powdered sandalwood dramatise the elegance of these women. They also use kohl or indigo to denote their tribal affiliation with a line and several dots on their chins.

108

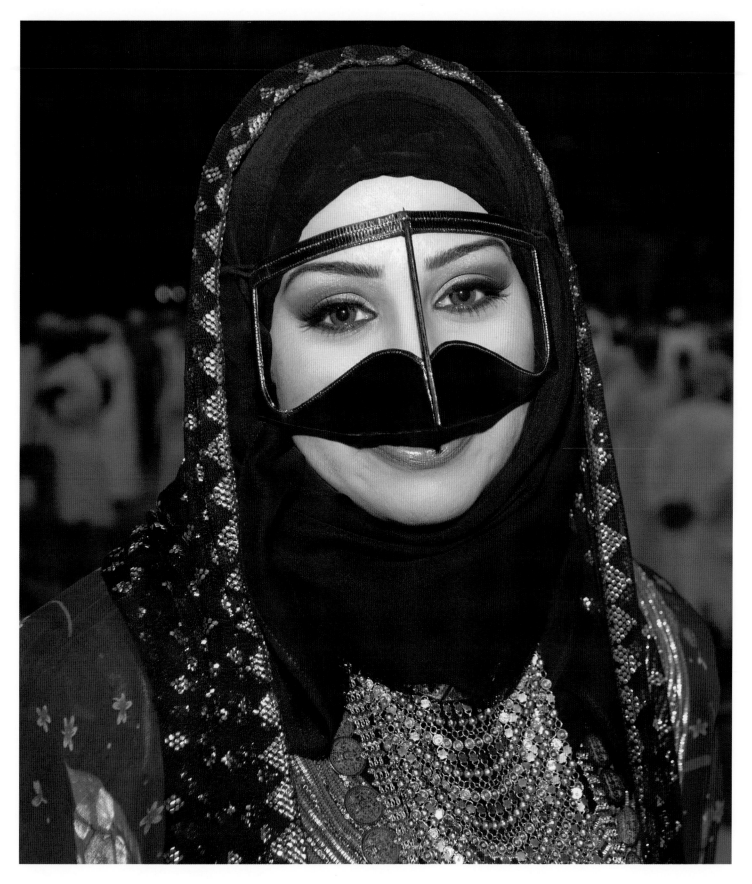

This spread: Small in size but large in character, this house is used by a family in Wadi Tiwi to drink tea or coffee, or enjoy dinner, after working in their date plantation.

Following spread: A schoolboy in the Sharqiyah Sands, left, waiting for the bus. The little boy in the centre, holding a traditional wooden stick, has his feet adorned with henna; and, to the right, a colourful wooden door frames unselfconscious Omani children.

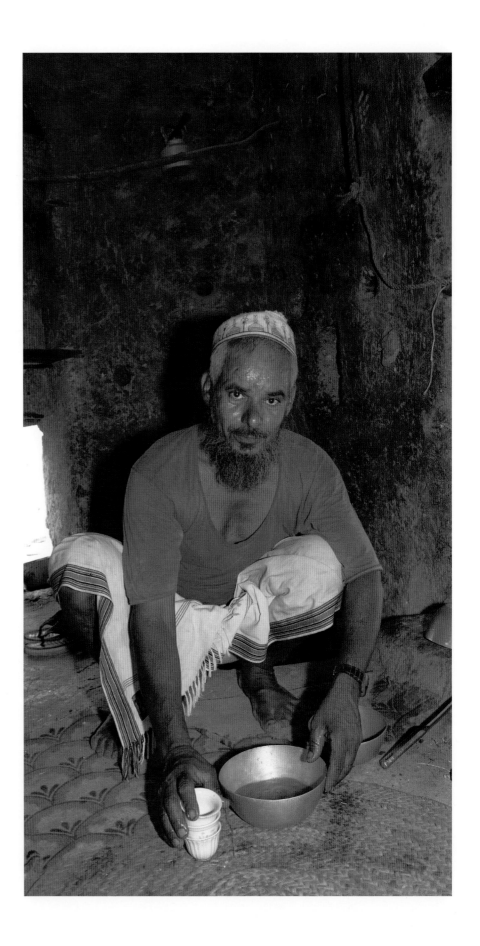

112

Above: The famous old mosque at Ja'lan Bani Bu Ali, at the eastern edge of the Sharqiyah Sands, dates back to the Omayyad Dynasty of between 661 and 750 AD. This mosque is famous for its more than 50 domes and is one of Oman's few remaining ancient mosques.

Left: A beautifully renovated small castle in the village of Rawda.

The region of Sharqiyah (which means 'eastern' in Arabic) maintains its traditional industries, including the crafting of both the traditional *khanjar*, above, and model boats, left, which are painstakingly made for exhibitions. The full-size versions of traditional dhows are constructed today as they always have been, with a hammer, bow drill, saw, chisel, awl, plane and caulking iron, and without the use of electricity or modern equipment. Indian teak is typically used to craft the hull, while the ribs are made locally from various types of wood, including *sidr, qart* and *sarar*.

Above: The love of horses can be seen in the way Omanis adorn their chargers with neck ornaments, silver bridles, sweat covers; silver collar pieces and decorated reins. Colourful parades are held during annual horse races and shows at the Royal Stables, and throughout the country, especially during religious or national occasions and festivals.

Right: The crowd occupies every conceivable vantage point to watch the camel races in Sharqiyah. The races provide an ideal time to socialise as well.

Inland, the desert area of Al-Wusta region is home to the Arabian oryx, Nubian ibex, Arabian gazelle, caracal, lynx, desert rabbit, fox, mountain goat and more than 130 different bird species. The coastal area features wide bays, caves and inlets. Dolphins can be seen offshore and both migratory birds and resident sea birds add to the natural attractions of the area. The coastline is punctuated by several ship wrecks, such as this contemporary wreck at Ra's Madrakah and the wreck of a traditional dhow at Ra's Ad Duqm.

Along Al-Wusta's beaches you'll be able to find hundreds, maybe thousands of flamingoes. Greater flamingoes are spectacular, particularly in flight, when their red and black wings are revealed in an array of glory. The pink plumage of a flamingo is caused by ingested organic compounds, which are found in shallow water.

Above: The Arabian oryx, a member of the antelope family, is specially adapted to life in the harsh desert environment. It can live for a considerable time without drinking water as it gets considerable moisture from vegetation. Usually found in small herds led by a dominant male or alpha female, the Arabian oryx was hunted to extinction in the Sultanate by 1972. Starting in 1979, it was reintroduced in the Jiddat al-Harasiis, as part of a project directly supported by His Majesty Sultan Qaboos bin Said; and its numbers are currently increasing. The Arabian Oryx Sanctuary in the Jiddat al-Harasiis is now a UNESCO World Heritage Site.

Left: The Arabian gazelle is also protected in the Arabian Oryx Sanctuary and plentiful herds of this beautiful animal can now be found in the Jiddat al-Harasiis.

Far left: Some 24 species of reptile have been recorded in the Jiddat al-Harasiis, the largest of which is the grey monitor lizard, which feeds primarily on other lizards and insects. Pictured is the yellow-spotted agama (*Trapelus Flavimaculatus*), an inhabitant of the area.

For centuries the camel has been the Bedouin's champion and companion. It is one of the few species able to withstand the rigours of desert travel, because it can store water in its blood and nutrients in its body, regurgitating food when necessary. There are many breeds of camel in Oman and all are lightweight, fast and relatively small compared to others in the Gulf region. Camel racing is a very popular sport and a good specimen can bring enormous wealth to its owner.

A fossilised reef of rudists near Saiwan belongs to an era when the area was covered by a shallow sea. Rudists were bivalve marine molluscs often found together in large banks, which developed in the tropical waters during the Cretaceous period around 100-million-years ago. They possessed two shells, one shaped like a large beaker and the other acted as a close-fitting lid. Their shells could grow to a great size, sometimes more than a metre in length.

A rock garden at Ra's Ad Duqm. Here the landscape is scattered with rocks, spectacular in form and colour. The result of erosion, the colours vary from deep purple to off white, and everything in between.

Dhofar, spanning a third of the Sultanate of Oman, is located at the southern end of the country and is dramatically different from Oman's other regions and, indeed, from the rest of the Gulf. It benefits from the annual Indian monsoon, locally known as the *Khareef*, which occurs between July and September. With an abundance of water brought by the *Khareef*, Dhofar's landscape in the Salalah area on the southern coast is transformed into lush greenery with waterfalls, meandering streams and lakes. The area is engulfed in fog and mist creating an ethereal atmosphere. Salalah is the region's administrative capital and Oman's second-largest city with an airport and large container port development area. Further inland, the landscape features vary from the high dunes of the Rub al-Khali, to many unexplored caves and numerous sinkholes within mountain valleys. Dhofar is steeped in legend, two of the more famous concern the lost city of Ubar and the Queen of Sheba. Some believe that the ruins at Shisr are the fabled city of Ubar and that the excavations at Khor Rori have revealed the palace of the Queen of Sheba. The coastal fringe of Dhofar, pictured here, is touched by the *Khareef*. The surface winds encourage an upwelling of colder waters in the Indian Ocean, which cool the overlying, moisture-laden air. Seas are high during the *Khareef*, particularly at the Whale's Mouth near Al-Mughsayl, west of Salalah, which attracts numerous tourists intent on visiting the blowholes where jets of water are forced through narrow vents in the limestone rocks.

Rakhyut in the Dhofar region, above, is a small village at the end of a steep, forested gorge overlooking a beautiful beach. The village is almost as far south as you can go before reaching the Republic of Yemen. To the left, this rocky coastline is just off the new, tarmac road east from Sadah.

136

Above: Traditional Dhofari houses in Mirbat, constructed from quarried stone and plastered in clay, are typically decorated with motifs in bas relief.

Top left: Repairing fishing nets at the Khareef Festival.

Bottom left: A local coffee shop in Taqah near Salalah. Village elders often sit together in a circle and discuss the news of the day.

Above: Salalah has an abundant and diverse range of fruit and vegetables, including papayas, bananas, guavas, oranges, custard apples, avocados and coconuts. Most of the fruit farms are located at Dahariz, in the eastern part of Salalah, and, during the *Khareef*, tourists are welcomed to specially created stalls with thatched roofs and coconut-palm decoration – an enchanting sight.

Right: The *Khareef* transforms the countryside into a veritable garden, such as in Wadi Ayn Athum pictured here. It is a good time to visit Salalah and take in the exciting Khareef Festival, the cultural highlight of the season.

Above: An Omani woman and her son sell candy floss at the side of the road during the *Khareef*, when the area becomes inundated with visitors from other Gulf countries.

Left: Goats on a misty morning in Dhofar. Kept enclosed at night, the goats are released first thing in the morning by their goatherds to graze on the abundant vegetation of the *Khareef* season.

Above left: *Calotropis Procera*, a plant from the milkweed family, locally known as *shakr* and, in English, as Sodom's Apple. This African milkweed species has a native range that covers not only Oman but also the whole of south-west Asia. Goats and camels avoid this plant because of its poisonous milk.

Above right: This parasitic, yellow broomrape is known locally as *thanoon* or a desert hyacinth, and is a member of the *Orobanchaceae* family.

Top left: The baobab, *Adansonia Digitata*, leafless for nine months of the year, can grow up to 25 metres tall and lives for several thousand years. This strange tree is the stuff of Afro-Arabian legend: "The devil plucked up the baobab, thrust its branches into the earth and left its roots in the air".

Top right: The succulent desert rose, a member of the oleander family, grows in the wild on bushes from two to three metres wide. It has beautiful pink flowers that bloom between Spring and Autumn.

Bottom right and left: Frankincense, a resin hardened from the sap of the frankincense tree, is a centrepiece in Oman's heritage. In Dhofar, the *Boswellia Sacra*, or Sacred Frankincense, produces oleo gum resin of the highest quality. Frankincense was used widely in the past and, at times, was prized as highly as gold. Omanis still use it today, burning it on glowing charcoal to fumigate rooms and clothing, and blending it in local perfumes.

Weavers from the village of Shuwaymiyah work on the strong, coiled desert-palm Bedu basketry, which is usually decorated with dark strips of goat or camel leather to provide a striking contrast to the beige palm material.